yoga and grief

a compassionate journey
toward healing

By Gloria Drayer
and Kathleen Doherty

BALBOA.
PRESS

A DIVISION OF HAY HOUSE

Cover photography by: Barbara Conley

Cover design, interior design by: Carolyn Flynn

Balboa Press books may be ordered through booksellers or by contacting:

Balboa Press
A Division of Hay House
1663 Liberty Drive
Bloomington, IN 47403
www.balboapress.com
1 (877) 407-4847

ISBN: 978-1-4525-9120-9 (sc)
ISBN: 978-1-4525-9121-6 (e)

Library of Congress Control Number: 2014901472

Printed in the United States of America.

Balboa Press rev. date: 5/05/2014

dedication

To my mom, Tillie, for giving me life and showing me grace in dying;

and to yoga, which supports me through the sorrow and joys of my life.

Gloria Drayer

To Jon, with love and gratitude, and to my family for their love and support.

Kathleen Doherty

table of contents

Foreword 1

Introduction   3

Notes on Grief   9

Breathing Techniques   14

Yoga Postures   18
Chair   22
Standing   30
Floor   39
Resting   45
Longer Practice   50

Chanting   64

Meditation   74
Guided Meditation   80

Seeking Comfort   84

Healing Rituals 85

Final Words   91

Resources   92

Acknowledgments   93

About the Authors   94

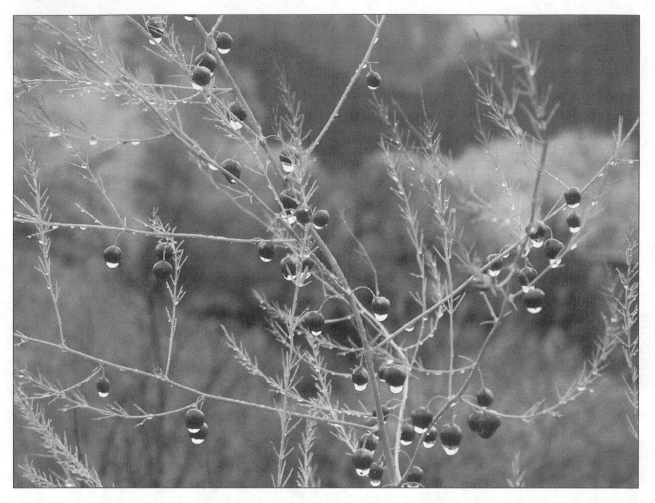

Blessed are those who mourn, for they shall be comforted.

Matthew 5:4

ENGLISH STANDARD VERSION

foreword

Grief comes in waves.

When you have lost someone you love, the sadness is a powerful undertow in your life. On the surface, the core structure of your life may seem much as you have always known it. Yet this is incongruent with the deep truth within: Someone you love is missing. You carry within you the profound sense that ground beneath your feet has shifted, as though you are lost in a vast ocean, far from dry land.

You hold the dissonance of the thought that the person is missing, yet the one you love occupies an immense space in your heart, mind, and soul. More than you could ever imagine.

Your beloved one is gone. The stark realization of this can bowl you over when you least expect it. The magnitude of grief is often beyond our ability to articulate it or describe it to another person. You really have to be there, in the grief-body, to know and remember. Even if ... even if you have been there before.

During the year my mother was dying, my sisters and I came to call the sluggish and clumsy ways we operated as "grief-brain." We gave each other grace because we understood that a good portion of our thoughts and our ways of interacting was consumed by the sadness that we were losing her.

She was irreplaceable. And we would have to let her go.

Grief is the most visceral of human emotions. I am convinced of that. It holds you in a physical grip, occupying your mind, anchoring itself in your heart, and rooting deep in your soul. It demands that you examine the deepest, darkest and most beautiful parts of yourself. It may be the most palpable emotion humans can feel.

Yoga proved essential for me in the long journey of losing my mother, for its power to ground me in my body, clear my crowded mind, and soothe my soul. Yoga made me brave and strong when I needed to be brave for my mother, when I needed to assure her she could face her death, and I could face losing her.

"Stay. Alive," she whispered to me as she gasped for her last breaths. "Stay. Alive!" she repeated, so I would not forget.

Yoga keeps me alive. The sheer discipline of yoga – the strength of its gentle wisdom, executed with mindfulness and compassionate nonjudgment, its balance of effort and surrender – is a map for staying alive. Yoga can guide you through your journey with grief, reconstituting you with new mettle. With each practice, you are made new. The practice can fortify you with a renewed and vigorous spiritual force.

Gloria Drayer brings a gentle, calm, and compassionate spirit to the practice she teaches, and you'll find that spirit infuses every page (or screen) of this book. She knows that when you care for someone, you give, and when you give of your spirit, as you do when you love someone through their journey with dying, you need the gentle sustenance that yoga provides.

If you are facing a loss or processing the aftermath of a loss, I urge you to use this book as your beacon of light on the shore.

When the undertow of grief roils at your ankles in these uncertain waters, use this book to build a yoga practice and find your way back to the light and love that you know to be the truth. Trust, as I did, that Gloria will guide you home.

~ *Carolyn Flynn, October 2013, co-author of "The Complete Idiot's Guide to Mindfulness" and "The Complete Idiot's Guide to Creative Visualization"*

introduction

Those who grieve often feel as if they are viewing the world from the wrong end of a telescope. In this strange and constricted space, time slows, priorities change, and daily routine feels impossible. Some days even getting out of bed requires more energy than we can generate.

And yet, life goes on.

People go to work, bills get paid, and your neighbor still walks his dog each morning at sunrise.

We all expect to grieve at some time in our lives. What we cannot prepare for is how we will feel when faced with loss.

Our simple hope in writing this book is to share with you what we have learned to help you take care of yourself based upon our own grief experiences.

kathleen

Ironically, toward the end of our collaboration on this book, I found myself dealing with a catastrophic medical event. I did not have Gloria's years of experience and discipline to help me face this sudden loss. In basic terms what I needed first was to "just calm down." I am grateful for the support of family and friends but it was the alone moments, the times when fears loom large and the mind is full of questions for which there are no good answers, that I knew the work on this book was an unexpected gift. I relied mainly on meditation and journaling during my treatment and recovery, and listening to chant is what helped me to sleep at night. As I got stronger I was able to resume yoga and still rely on the gentle practices found in this book.

gloria

My mother died of a brain tumor in 2006. When I look back, I know that the grieving began at the time of her diagnosis, more than a year prior to her death. During her illness my siblings and I were able to participate a lot in her care giving. We bathed her, fixed her meals, and rubbed her feet – anything to make her feel comfortable. It was natural for me then to turn to my yoga practice to find calm and inner strength. It helped me be centered and connected to my mother's final needs. I meditated in the morning before she woke up; but often there was not enough time to do a full yoga series, so my practice was simple and restorative.

I have always adhered to the advice, "Believe in what comforts you." Yoga kept me calm and healthy. I could simply be with my mother and not feel like I needed to try to fix or change the situation.

Surviving deep loss marks you forever, but suffering can be transformed. The techniques you will find in this book – yoga, meditation, breathing, chanting, and the use of ritual – allow moments of respite for the body and the mind.

types of loss

Death of a loved one

Divorce or end of a relationship

Betrayal

Loss of faith

Loss of a job or home

Loss of a pet

Loss of health or function

Loss of safety

No one can judge which might be the "worst" loss or how a person should react. Grief is what it is — a spectrum with many bands and varying intensity, an energy with its own ebb and flow. Loss can be devastating. The changes to the body and soul, the heart and mind, are painful. Of that we can be assured.

who can benefit from this book? Anyone experiencing

a need for relief from the physical, spiritual, and emotional toil of grief

Anyone who is caregiver to a person in transition

Anyone of any age regardless of the degree of physical fitness

Gloria realized that the yoga techniques that helped her during her mother's illness and death could be used to help others regardless of their stage of grief. Much of what you find in this book comes from her experience with her mother, the work she has done with clients, and from the grief workshops she has given over the years.

how to use this book This

book is an easy reference, so you can take from it any part that works for you. Some may find the yoga postures are what they need. Others may find chanting or breathing techniques relieve deep sadness. Still, others may find that relief through meditation. If you wish, skip around through the chapters. Pick and choose sections that appeal you. Remember to take care of yourself in ways that seem best to you.

The yoga postures included here may be familiar to those of you who have practiced yoga. But even if you have never done so, these postures are easy to follow. This system of yoga can fit into any lifestyle and any amount of time. You do not have to spend days or even a single hour to see results. However, like anything else, the more you practice, the more you will benefit. You will be able to see results if you make a commitment to follow through, especially in times of distress or sadness. It is not in the *doing*, it is in the *being* with yoga that can alter grief.

benefits of yoga

Lowering blood pressure
Strengthening bones and muscles
Improving flexibility and balance
Increasing lung capacity
Decreasing stress
Improving mood and concentration

Along with the sections dealing with yoga and meditation, we have included chapters suggesting opportunities for release through participation in various rituals and complementary healing.

Whether you are sorting things out on your own or in a community, ritual is a powerful transformational tool for dealing with grief.

This is a journey toward well-being. It is not a competition. No one is keeping score. So, please be aware of your own needs, and be compassionate with your own situation. Do not feel discouraged if you find that you cannot participate just yet. Sometimes the act of sitting up a little straighter and focusing on one full breath — its inhalation and exhalation — is all we can manage in a day. Finally, taking care of ourselves involves being aware of, and discussing with your healthcare provider ahead of time, any conditions that would prevent or limit physical activity. The same holds true in the event of prolonged or incapacitating grief. You may need to seek outside guidance. These healing processes are not meant as a substitute for professional help. To put it simply, sometimes it is necessary to recognize that you cannot do everything by yourself.

notes on grief

Grief is a space, a void, unknown territory.

The journey can be complicated and disorienting, and it can rob us of our health and well-being. At times when we think we are doing okay, grief can surge up like a great wave from within, knocking us down, making us stumble and fall.

Those who grieve know all too well the burden of a heavy heart. Time slows and we wonder how much sadness a heart can really take.

Can you trust that you won't grieve forever? Can you let yourself believe that the light within you is greater than the darkness that now surrounds you? There may be the moments when your inner voice, your soul, directs you.

Listen.

Allow yourself to be guided, to feel a connection to life. Maybe even allow yourself to feel gratitude. You may be led to work in the garden or, perhaps, to sit in a park and listen to the birds. The sadness may very well return, but you have given yourself a moment of respite and you will trust that it can happen again.

There is no instant cure for grief, no timetable that tells you when you can expect to be back to normal. "Normal" certainly will be redefined. There are, however, subtle ways to ground yourself, to redirect your energy and to feel some sense of relief as you journey through this process. Not so long ago, grieving was an event filled with ritual and shared deeply by one homogenous community. Now, many are left to sort it out on their own because a society of multiplicity no longer supports grieving. Too often, we encounter a certain impatience with grief. It's too personal and awkward. When so much of our daily life is hurried, it is easy to view grief as something for which we no longer have time. If we are fortunate, we find community, those who can patiently stand by us without the expectation that within a certain time we must get over feeling bad.

As you read this book, we implore you to seek a new balance in your life between the external forces that fight against your grief process and your internal sense of what you need to grieve. Learn to pay attention to the nuances of how you feel. Take the time to get to know your particular way of experiencing grief. There will be days when your yoga practice and meditation will soothe you. Other days, you may have to call someone and say, "I'm feeling really sad, and I need to talk." This simple acknowledgment can be a source of comfort and release. Learn to feel the grief and acknowledge it.

We know there are many ways to deal with grief and loss. From the *Yoga Simple and Sacred* Grief Workshops, Gloria is reminded of a woman who had been in psychotherapy for several years and who said she got more out of a three-hour workshop than she did from years of "talking it out." Gloria feels that the woman's prior work helped her get to a place where she was receptive to yoga movement, breathing, and meditation. Another student said she did not want to hold grief in her body because she was getting sick frequently. Yoga practice helped her on her road to healing by showing her how to reduce stress, become peaceful and bring her body to a more balanced state.

When someone we love is dying, we often hold back our own emotions and postpone grieving – only to suffer the effects later. We can notice changes in our posture – physically from the exhausting work of care giving, but also in emotional posture. When we are hurt, it is a natural reaction to close off our hearts to

protect ourselves from further suffering. Even our breathing changes, along with our mental processes. We may be depressed and lethargic, or agitated, and unable to concentrate or sleep. However, if we can find a few minutes to meditate, incorporate a heart-opening posture or a breathing exercise, these methods can help re-establish our equilibrium and shift the energy to a place of peace.

In this book we talk about finding various ways to *shift the energy*. But what exactly does that mean? We know that everything in the Universe is made up of energy. We can distinguish types of energy, but we probably don't think about how we can transform the life force within us. When we are caught up in grief, our energy changes and we become unbalanced. This change can manifest in different ways, from incapacitating sadness to agitation or lethargy. Whatever you care to call it, you know that it hurts. The question then becomes, "What can you do to shift that energy to a more balanced and peaceful state?"

Along with shifting the energy, another term we use is *mindfulness*. To be mindful is to have awareness. It is a state of acceptance without feelings of attachment, judgment, or resistance. To practice mindfulness is to feel grounded and to have balance in our lives.

Neither of these concepts is new. They are at the core of many spiritual practices, and they are the foundation on which this book is based. Putting these concepts to work involves trying techniques that may be "outside of the box," tools that you might not think to access in the midst of your grief.

This book does not offer an easy solution for grief. People process life events at their own pace and usually find what they need when the time is right. Methods to shift the energy depend upon the person and what works best for him or her. Yoga helps you concentrate as you move from one posture into another.

Breathing exercises can change the way you feel in a matter of minutes. Walking and meditation can bring about the same effects. Other times, you may find that working a little longer, concentrating on a task, or spending time with people gives you relief.

As your life goes on, surely you will face other losses. A yoga discipline can provide a lifelong foundation for centering and relief during these times.

Everyone's experience is unique. Transformation takes however long it takes. Yoga eases. It will strengthen you, but it does not shorten the journey.

Just as the activities of the mind influence the breath,
so does the breath influence our state of mind.

T.K.V. Desikachar

INDIAN YOGA MASTER

breathing techniques

Conscious breathing is a powerful tool that can enhance mental and emotional clarity. Its purpose is to invite a state of balance to the body and mind. Breathing consciously and mindfully can promote calmness and/or energy by focusing awareness on our breath. Each breathing technique has its own benefits.

If you are new to yogic breathing, start off slowly. We suggest practicing abdominal breathing at first, and use only one breathing technique at a time. This will help you become familiar with the techniques and their benefits and how you can incorporate them into your day.

The following exercises are done best on an empty stomach. Wear loose, comfortable, non-restrictive clothing. If you find yourself needing to do a breathing technique at a time when you are not prepared, allow your practice to adapt to your circumstances.

As everyone has different needs and abilities, some may find it helpful to find a yoga practitioner with experience in breathing techniques to provide guidance. For most of these exercises, you should be sitting in a chair or on the floor with a straight spine so that the diaphragm is not compressed and the air flows freely in and out of the lungs. As the breath enters the lungs, it moves the diaphragm downward, which expands the abdomen. For all the breathing techniques included here, breathe in and out through the nostrils unless you are experiencing nasal congestion, in which case, mouth breathing may be used.

Please note: If during the practice you experience agitation, shortness of breath or lightheadedness, simply stop the exercise and resume your regular breathing. You can always come back to these exercises but do them gradually; perhaps focusing on the exhalation, as this is generally easier for most people, or doing fewer rounds, or holding the breath for a shorter period.

types of breathing

Abdominal Breath: Place hands on your abdomen one above the other and inhale the breath deep into your abdomen. On the exhalation, move your navel toward your spine. Repeat six times. When you become more comfortable with all the postures, you may want to practice abdominal breathing throughout this series, remembering to inhale and exhale through your nose.

Three-part Breath: Begin in a comfortable seated position. Place your left hand on your abdomen and your right hand on your upper chest. Inhale into your chest, then your ribs and then your abdomen. Exhale in reverse order: from your abdomen, your ribs, and then your chest. Notice the movement of your hands as your breath enters and leaves your body. Begin with two sets of six repetitions. Pause after your first set and take a few normal breaths, and then begin the second set.

Throat Breathing: You may incorporate this into all of the other breathing techniques in this chapter. Throat breathing aids in the quality of attentiveness. It keeps the mind engaged and calm.

At first, practice this only on your exhalation. Allow the back of your throat to constrict, narrowing the air passage so that you are making a sound like the ocean. If you are unsure about this, try opening your mouth and pretending that you are fogging a mirror with your breath. Listen to the sound. Now try

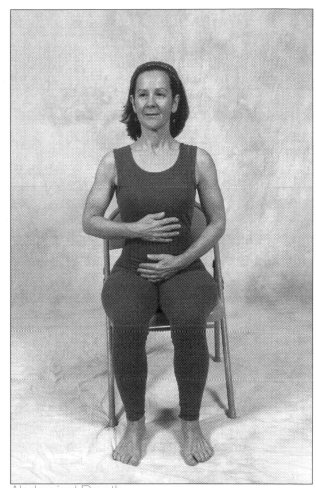
Abdominal Breath

to repeat the sound, but this time, close your mouth. When you are comfortable, add it to the inhalation. Eventually try to make your breath longer and smoother. Do two sets of six repetitions.

Counting the Breath: You can add this to either Abdominal or Throat Breathing. Simply count to yourself as your breath comes in and, again, as it goes out. Gradually try to extend your exhalation a couple of seconds longer than your inhalation. For example, inhale to the count of four and exhale to the count of six. This can be either relaxing or energizing depending upon whether you focus on the exhalation (calming) or the inhalation (energizing).

Focus on the Exhalation: This technique produces a calm and relaxed feeling. Use Throat Breathing, allowing your inhalation to enter freely. As you exhale half your breath, pause, then exhale the remaining breath. If you find that your breath is coming out too fast, don't take in so much breath so you can slow down your exhalation. This is nice to do in the evening, or when you are experiencing stress, anxiety, or sleeplessness.

With every breath I take today,

I vow to be awake;

and every step I take,

I vow to take with a grateful heart –

So I may see with eyes of love

into the hearts of all I meet,

to ease their burden when I can

and touch them with a smile of peace.

Anonymous

yoga postures

Perhaps many of you who are reading this have no experience or understanding of yoga. We can assure you that it doesn't matter. What is important is that yoga can help anywhere along the spectrum of grief and loss. It can bestow calmness and strength, and help you come out the other side as whole as possible.

Yoga is a 5,000-year-old practice. Contrary to what many people think, it is not a religion. In its simplest form, it combines physical poses, breathing exercises, and meditation. It also includes guidelines for healthy living and spirituality.

For many people, yoga can be a method of complementing other spiritual or philosophical beliefs. The origin of the word "yoga" means "to unite" or "to join." To this end, yoga seeks oneness with the Universe, which in turn, leads to an appreciation of the interconnectedness of all existence.

At various times in our lives and for various reasons, we face the realization that the exact thing we don't *want* to do is what we *need* to do. Some days we can easily convince ourselves that we don't have the energy to get out of bed, get dressed, or tend to body and home. We prefer to be left alone with our heartache.

It's OK.

Feel what you are feeling; yet, recognize that soon you will need to find ways to help yourself feel better.

We hope in this book you will find support to help you remain mindful and centered in spite of the inevitable stress that loss produces. Learning to trust yourself in the midst of strong and painful feelings is difficult, but there are ways to nurture yourself in the process.

The yoga series go from active to restorative postures. Certain postures will help support you when the grief seems unbearable; others help to relieve depression or move your body from a state of stagnant energy. Some days will dictate a calming practice and other days, an energizing one. If you don't have much time, perhaps you can manage a session of breathing techniques, a short meditation, or even a few yoga postures at your desk. In time you will know what you need and how to get the most benefit from your practice. With a little investment of time, you will begin to feel better. This is not meant to take away the grief but to aid and comfort you as you experience it.

Gloria has found that most people experiencing grief need a more calming yoga practice. The postures selected here can help calm the mind and reduce stress. In addition, they can facilitate the expansion of the lungs and chest, which may feel constricted. When we are depressed or stressed, we tend to hunch over, causing us to not breathe as deeply which, in turn, makes us more depressed because of the lack of oxygen to the brain — a vicious cycle! Therefore, moving and lengthening the spine to keep it fluid and flexible is also important.

We suggest gentle movements because in the time of grief and vulnerability, these practices are less demanding. Most people will be able to do each of the series in this chapter, and modifications can be made to nearly all of them to accommodate any special needs or physical limitations. For example, if you can't do certain floor postures, you can modify them into a standing posture or use a chair. Postures that place the head lower than the heart should be avoided by those with hypertension or glaucoma. Those with back sensitivities may wish to refrain from certain postures that place

stress on the spine, such as Chair Twist, Seated Spinal Movements and Back Bends. If you are uncertain, please check with your health professional before beginning any exercise.

The physical practice of yoga involves postures that restore our sense of balance. Often when we experience stress, we live in our minds and disconnect from our bodies. For this reason, it is important to do physical movement to shift and rebalance the energy.

Before you begin your practice, you may want to express an intention. This can help set the tone of the practice. For example: "I do this practice for my mind to be calm and my body to remain healthy…." Observe how you feel in each posture, and how the posture makes you feel after you do it. Are you moving the body in a gentle and compassionate way?

If you are able, commit to a minimum of 10 minutes of yoga a day, especially when you are feeling really overwhelmed or sad. Even if you can only do the breathing exercises alone, you will benefit. Use the time you have available and go with what gives you comfort. As your practice builds, you may wish to add chanting and mudras/gestures to these postures, or hold the postures for a longer time. For those of you experienced with yoga or who need more, a longer practice is included at the end of this chapter.

Each series starts with a breathing technique. Typically, you inhale and exhale through the nose. If you have nasal congestion, you can breathe through the mouth. As you become more familiar with the all of the postures, you can gradually increase the time you hold them by staying for one or two breaths longer. Begin the breath slightly before initiating each of the movements, moving slowly so the breath will also slow down. Complete each series in the order given for continuity and balance. You may do all of the postures in one series and add more if you have the time. It is only by **doing** that you will begin to feel a change.

props In most yoga traditions, props are used. Here they are not required, though you will notice that a blanket or a chair can be used with some of the resting postures. In addition, a yoga eye bag or a cloth to cover your eyes may enhance your relaxation at the end of your practice. Use props if you are used to them. Remember that you don't need anything but yourself to do yoga. Adapt your postures to your circumstances. For example, if you are at work and having a difficult moment, back away from what you are doing, and do some arm movements and deep breathing. Breathing techniques are well suited to the times you are away from your usual place of practice.

rest Rest is an important part of yoga. At the end of a series, rest gives you the opportunity to integrate the benefits of the practice.

No effort is wasted and no gain is ever lost when on this path;
even a little practice will shelter you from sorrow
and protect you from the greatest fear.

Bhagavad Gita
HINDU SCRIPTURE

chair postures

Sit toward the front of the chair with a straight spine. Your back should be away from the back of the chair. Place your feet flat on the floor, comfortably apart. If your feet don't touch the floor, place a folded blanket under them. In all the postures, begin the breath slightly before you start the movement. Take two breaths as you transition from one posture to another.

1. Abdominal Breathing: Note: All breathing is through the nose. Place hands on your abdomen one above the other and inhale the breath deep into your abdomen. On the exhalation, move your navel toward your spine. Repeat six times. When you become more comfortable with all the postures, you may want to practice abdominal breathing throughout this series, remembering to inhale and exhale through your nose.

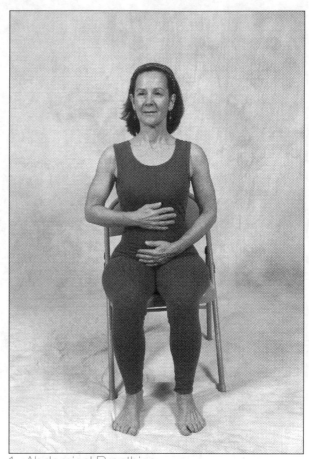
1. Abdominal Breathing

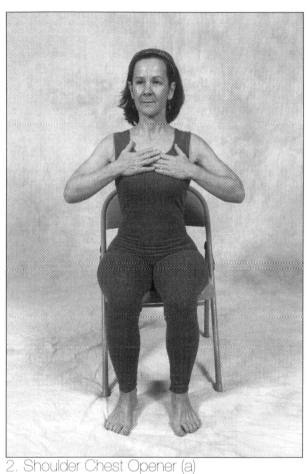

2. Shoulder Chest Opener (a)

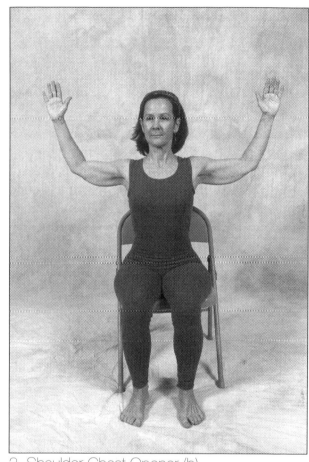

2. Shoulder Chest Opener (b)

2. Shoulder Chest Opener: Start with both hands at your chest. Inhale while slightly lifting your chest as you open your arms out to the side, elbows slightly bent. Exhale while bringing your hands back to your chest. Repeat four to six times.

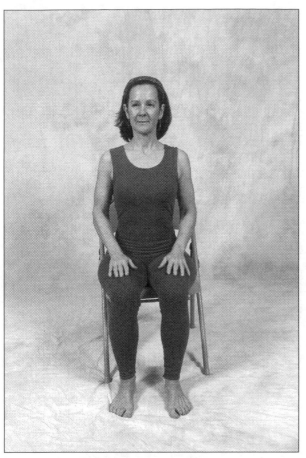

3. Arm and Leg Raises (a)

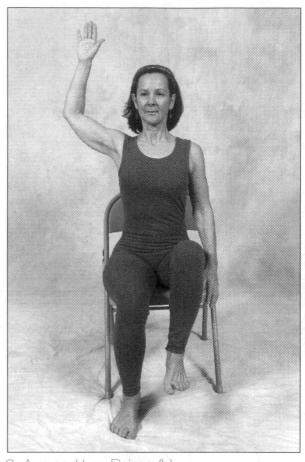

3. Arm and Leg Raises (b)

3. Arm and Leg Raises: Inhale as you lift your right arm and left leg. Make sure to keep your spine vertical. Exhale as you return to starting position. Alternate sides. Repeat four to six times. As you feel more comfortable in the posture, you can lift both your leg and arm higher, keeping your spine straight.

4. Chair Twist (a)

4. Chair Twist (b)

4. Chair Twist: Sit with your legs hip width apart. Inhale as you extend your arms out to the side, parallel to the floor. With your gaze following your left hand, exhale and begin to turn your trunk to the left, allowing your right hand to come toward your left shoulder. As you inhale, come back to center. Exhale and repeat, on the other side. Repeat each side three times. Remember to keep your back straight and your chin parallel to the floor.

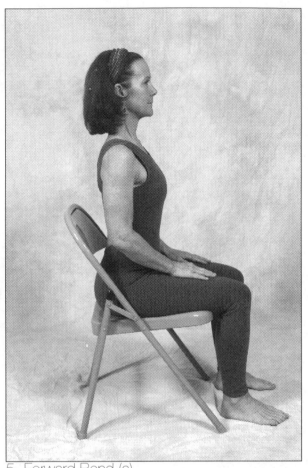

5. Forward Bend (a)

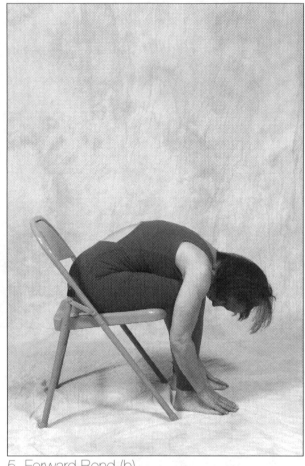

5. Forward Bend (b)

5. Forward Bend: Place hands on your lap. Exhale as you bend at the hips and allow your hands to slide down the front of your legs to a comfortable position. Keep your chin slightly tucked as you inhale, lifting your chest and coming up slowly, letting your hands slide up your legs. Repeat four to six times.

6. Seated Spinal Movements: Place hands on your lap. Exhale, as you bend at the hips, allowing your hands to slide down the front of your legs to a comfortable position. Keep your chin slightly tucked as you inhale and slightly lift your chest as you come only part way up. As you exhale, bend forward again. As you inhale, slowly come all the way up, lifting from your chest. Repeat three times.

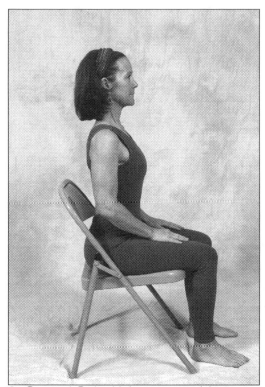

6. Seated Spinal Movements (a)

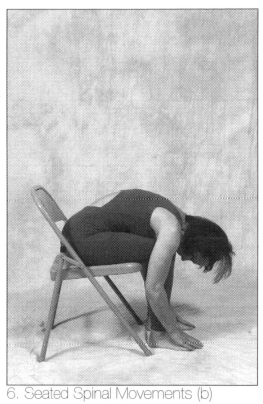

6. Seated Spinal Movements (b)

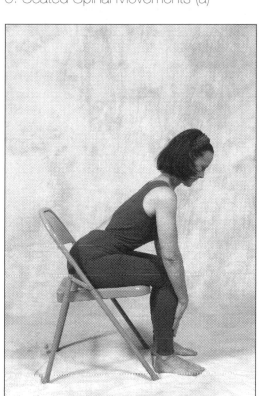

6. Seated Spinal Movements (c)

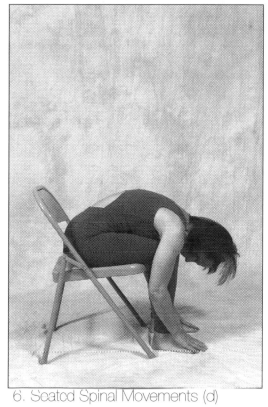

6. Seated Spinal Movements (d)

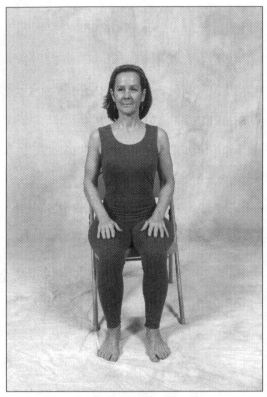

7. Neck and Shoulder Movements (a)

7. Neck and Shoulder Movements (b)

7. Neck and Shoulder Movements:
Place your hands in your lap, allowing your eyes and head to follow the movement of your hand. Inhale while raising your right arm up and out to the side, elbow slightly bent. Exhale slowly, placing your hand on your left shoulder. Inhale as you take your arm up and out to the side again. Exhale as you bring your arm back to your lap. Alternate sides, three times.

7. Neck and Shoulder Movements (c)

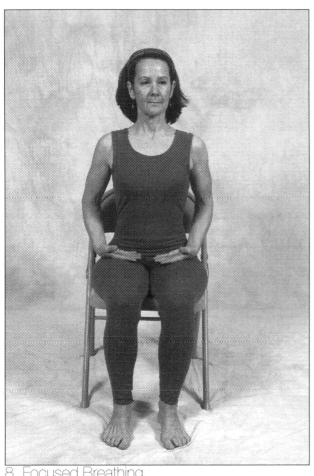

8. Focused Breathing

9. Rest

8. Focused Breathing: You can add this to either Abdominal or Throat Breathing (page 14-16). Simply count to yourself as your breath comes in, and again as it goes out. Gradually try to extend your exhalation a couple of seconds longer than your inhalation. For example, inhale to the count of four and exhale to the count of six. Complete ten to twelve rounds.

9. Rest: Rest in the chair with your eyes open or closed, hands in your lap with your palms facing up, allowing your body to relax completely. You also may relax lying on the floor, or choose any of the other Resting Postures found on page 45. Stay in your posture three to five minutes. When you come out of your resting posture, take a few integrating breaths and observe how you feel.

standing
postures Begin the

breath slightly before you start the movement.
Take two breaths as you transition from
one posture to another. Move slowly with
awareness from one posture to the next.

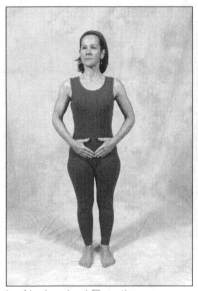

1. Abdominal Breath

2. Arm Raises (a)

2. Arm Raises (b)

1. Abdominal Breath: Place your hands on your abdomen and inhale the breath deep into your abdomen. On the exhalation, move your navel toward your spine. Repeat six times. When you become more comfortable with all the postures, you may want to practice abdominal breathing throughout this series, remembering to inhale and exhale through your nose.

2. Arm Raises: Stand with your arms by your sides. Inhale as you raise your arms out in front with bent elbows. Exhale to starting position. Repeat six times.

3. Balancing Posture (a)

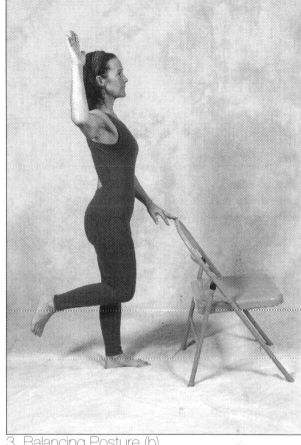

3. Balancing Posture (b)

3. Balancing Posture: Stand with your hands on the back of a chair. Inhale as you lift your right leg behind you and your right arm overhead having a slightly bent elbow. Exhale to starting position. Alternate sides, and repeat four more times. The last time, hold the posture for three breaths on each side. If you feel steady, you do not need to use the chair.

4. Spinal Movements (a)

4. Spinal Movements (b)

4. Spinal Movements: As you inhale, raise your arms. As you exhale, bend from the hips, allowing your hands to come to the seat of the chair. Keep your chin slightly tucked and inhale as you slightly lift your chest and come part way up. As you exhale, bend forward again. Inhale as you slowly come all the way up, lifting from your chest, and return to starting position. Repeat three times. This can be done without a chair by sliding your hands down the front of your legs.

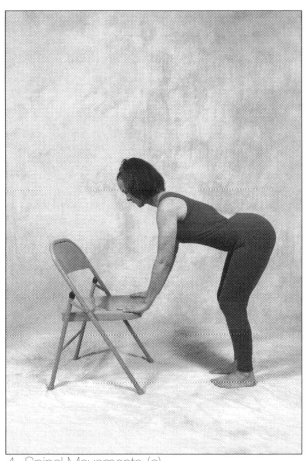

4. Spinal Movements (c)

4. Spinal Movements (d)

5. Warrior I (a)

5. Warrior I (b)

5. Warrior I: Step your right foot forward in a long stance. As you inhale, lift your arms up with elbows slightly bent while bending your front knee. Watch that your knee does not go forward over your ankle. Exhale as you lower your arms and straighten your front leg. Repeat six times. Return to starting position, and continue six times on the other side.

6. Forward Bend (a)

6. Forward Bend (b)

6. Forward Bend: Start with your arms at your sides. Inhale as you raise your arms up with bent elbows. Exhale as you bend at the hips and allow your hands to slide down the front of your legs to a comfortable position, letting your head relax. Keeping your chin slightly tucked, inhale as you lift your chest as you come up slowly, letting your hands slide up your legs. Repeat four to six times.

7. Standing Twist (a)

7. Standing Twist (b)

7. Standing Twist: Take a wide stance. As you inhale, raise your arms out to a T-position. With your gaze following your left hand, exhale and begin to turn your trunk to the left, allowing your right hand to come toward your left shoulder. As you inhale, come back to center. Exhale and repeat on the other side. Repeat each side three times. Remember to keep your back straight and your chin parallel to the floor.

7. Standing Twist (c)

8. Forward Bend (a)

8. Forward Bend (b)

8. Forward Bend: Inhale as you bring your arms up with bent elbows. Exhale as you bend at the hips and allow your hands to slide down the front of your legs to a comfortable position, letting your head relax. Keeping your chin slightly tucked, inhale lifting your chest as you come up slowly, letting your hands slide up your legs. Repeat four to six times.

9. Focused Breathing

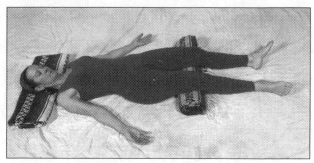

10. Rest

9. Focused Breathing: Lie on the floor with your knees bent, or sit in a chair. Take a moment to notice the effects of your Standing Practice. Inhale. Exhale, making your exhalation a little longer than your inhalation. Repeat ten times.

10. Rest: Lie on your back with your legs out in front of you or with knees bent, soles of the feet on the floor. Place arms at sides with palms up. Support your legs and head if you wish. Close your eyes. Allow your body to relax completely. Follow the natural movement of your breathing. If your mind wanders, return to focusing on your breath. Stay for at least five minutes. When it is time to come out of the posture, bend your knees and roll to your right side. Pause and take a few breaths. Using your left hand as support, come up slowly, keeping your neck relaxed. Sit for a moment, taking a few breaths. Notice the effects of your practice. You may also use Relaxation Posture or Legs on a Chair from the Resting Postures (page 45).

floor postures

Note: If you are not able to get down on the floor, omit these postures from your practice.

Start by kneeling on the floor and sitting back on your heels, or in a cross-legged position. Feel free to use the wall for back support. Let the breath begin slightly before each movement. The movement follows the breath. Take a few integrative breaths as you transition from one posture to another. Move slowly, and stay present for your experience.

1. Three-part Breath: Begin in a comfortable seated position. Place your left hand on your abdomen and your right hand on your upper chest. Inhale into your chest, then your ribs and then your abdomen. Exhale in reverse order: from your abdomen, your ribs, and then your chest. Notice the movement of your hands as your breath enters and leaves your body. Begin with two sets of six repetitions. Pause after your first set and take a few normal breaths, and then begin the second set.

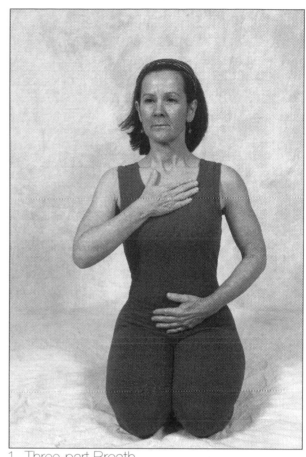
1. Three-part Breath

2. Spinal Movements (a)

2. Spinal Movements (c)

2. Spinal Movements (b)

2. Spinal Movements: Come to your hands and knees, shoulders in line with wrists. Use padding for your knees, if necessary. Exhale as you move your hips back toward — but not onto — your heels. As you inhale, lead with your chest, moving forward and coming into a slight back arch. Repeat six times.

3. Kneeling Forward Bend (a)

3. Kneeling Forward Bend (b)

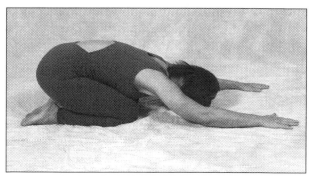

3. Kneeling Forward Bend (c)

3. Kneeling Forward Bend: Stand on your knees with your arms by your sides, knees placed hip width apart. Inhale as you raise your arms to the front. Exhale as you bring your hips toward your heels and bend your trunk forward, placing your hands and head on the floor in front of you. If your head does not touch the floor, use a pillow. Relax your elbows. Keep your chin slightly tucked. Inhale as you lift your arms and chest. Exhale as you lower your arms to your sides. Repeat six times. You can bring your hands to a chair or stool if you can't reach the floor.

4. Pelvic Lifts (a)

5. Knees In and Out (a)

4. Pelvic Lifts (b)

5. Knees In and Out (b)

4. Pelvic Lifts: Place feet slightly apart on the floor, hands resting on chest. Inhale as you open arms out to the side and press your feet into the floor, lifting your hips to a comfortable level. Exhale as you return to starting position. Gradually increase the height of the lift as you are able. Repeat six times.

5. Knees In and Out: Lift feet off the ground, placing hands on top of, or behind, your knees. Exhale as you draw your knees in toward your chest. Inhale as you return to starting position. Repeat six times.

6. Twist (a)

6. Twist (b)

6. Twist: Place feet on the floor hip width apart, arms out to your sides at shoulder height. Exhale as you gradually lower your knees a few inches to one side. Inhale as you return to center. Repeat to other side. With each repetition lower the knees a little further to the side. After a few repetitions you may turn your head to the opposite direction of your knees. Repeat six times, each side.

7. Leg Raises (a)

7. **Leg Raises:** Lie on your back with knees bent, feet off the floor, hands on knees. Inhale as you straighten your legs upward and move your arms overhead. Or, you may keep your hands behind your knees if you need the support. Exhale as you draw the knees toward the chest, hands on the knees, back to starting position. Repeat six times.

7. Leg Raises (b)

8. **Rest:** Lie on your back with your knees bent, soles of feet on the floor or with legs straight out on the floor. Place arms at sides with palms facing up. Close your eyes and allow your body to relax completely. Follow the natural movement of your breathing. If your mind wanders, bring it back to focusing on your breath. Stay for at least five minutes. When it is time to come out of the posture, bend your knees and slowly roll to your right side. Pause and take a few breaths. Using your left hand as support, come up slowly, keeping your neck relaxed. Sit for a moment, taking

8. Rest

a few breaths. Notice the effects of your floor practice. You may also use Relaxation Posture or Legs on a Chair (page 46).

resting postures

The following postures can be done at any time. They are helpful when you need to rest or restore yourself. Even a few minutes can recharge you and help you to get through the day. They can be done routinely before bedtime, or for those times when you might have trouble sleeping. Various postures mention taking neck support by using a blanket or towel. This keeps the neck straight and the chin perpendicular to the floor without hyperextending the neck. An eye bag or a small towel or cloth over your eyes can add to your sense of relaxation. Notice the effects of each posture.

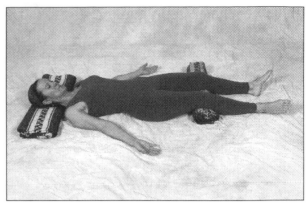

1. Relaxation Posture

1. Relaxation Posture: Place a bolster or two folded blankets under your knees and a rolled towel or blanket under your neck. Relax with your arms by your sides. If your mind needs quieting, add Throat Breathing or Counting the Inhalations and Exhalations. These are found in the Breathing Chapter (starting on page 14). Give yourself at least five minutes in this posture. When you are done, bend your knees and slowly roll to your right side. Pause. Using your left hand for support, slowly come up, keeping your neck relaxed. Sit for a moment and take a few breaths. Notice what you feel. This posture can be done at the end of any series as your resting posture.

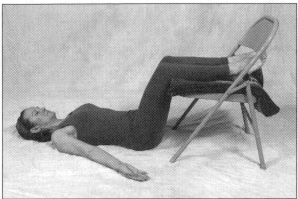

2. Legs on Chair

2. Legs on Chair: Place your legs on a chair, making sure the backs of your knees are comfortably supported on the chair. Some of you with longer legs may need to put your feet through the back of the chair or turn the chair sideways. Relax your arms by your sides. Inhale as you sweep your arms along the floor overhead with elbows softly bent. Exhale as you return your arms to starting position. Repeat six times.

If you would like to add a breathing technique, begin by inhaling freely, then exhale half the breath. Pause and exhale the other half. Complete six to eight rounds in this way. Then go back to your normal breathing pattern for at least five minutes. When you are done, remove your legs from the chair. Place your feet on the floor and slowly roll to your right side. Pause. Using your left hand for support, slowly come up, keeping your neck relaxed. Sit for a moment and take a few breaths. Notice what you feel. This posture can be used at the end of any other series as your resting posture.

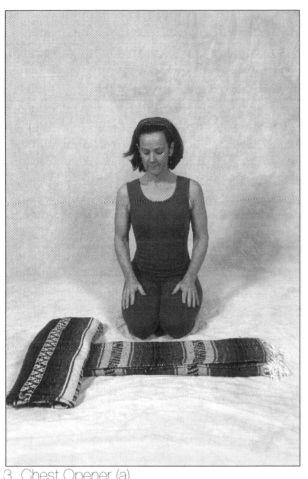

3. Chest Opener (a)

3. Chest Opener (b)

3. Chest Opener: Take a blanket folded in quarters, then fold in thirds lengthwise. Place another blanket at the top for your head, perpendicular to the first blanket. Sit on the bottom edge of the blanket with your knees bent, and lie down with the blanket centered between your shoulders. Re-adjust or add more neck support, if necessary. Your legs can be straight or bent with feet on the floor. Stay for five to seven minutes, focusing on a calming breath. Use Three Part Breath (page 15). To come out of the pose, gently roll to one side. Remove the blankets and return with your back flat on the floor. Be sure to complete this posture with the following counter posture:

4. Knees In and Out (a)

4. Knees In and Out (b)

4. Knees In and Out: Lift feet off the ground, placing hands on top of, or behind, your knees. Exhale as you draw your knees in toward your chest. Inhale as you return to starting position. Repeat six times.

5. Legs Up the Wall

5. Legs Up the Wall: Sit beside a wall. Lie back and swing your legs up the wall. Let your legs and torso form a right angle. Adjust your posture by bringing your buttocks close to the wall. If hamstrings are tight, bend your knees with your feet flat on the wall, or move your hips away from the wall. Rest five to ten minutes. You may use Throat Breathing and/or Three-part Breath (pages 14-16). To release, bend knees, roll to one side, and come up slowly. Sit for a few moments and take a few breaths. Notice how you feel.

Variation: Take legs into a V-shape, or bring the soles of your feet together, knees out to the sides, in Bound Angle Posture.

bedtime

Sleep is the foundation for a healthy life. It boosts the immune system and gives the body the opportunity to restore itself from the damage caused each day by stress. During sleep the body goes into repair mode regenerating skin, muscle, blood, and brain cells. Sleep deprivation affects every area of your life including your health, stamina, and relationships.

Yoga can help with sleep disturbance, but it is important to choose a less active practice before you go to bed. Any of Resting, Floor or Chair series, along with calming breaths, especially Abdominal Breathing (page 14) can help the mind and the body prepare for sleep.

Meditation also can be used to produce deep relaxation prior to sleep. Research indicates that the active process of meditation causes the body to "unwind," calming the mind and enabling you to fall into a peaceful state of sleep. Feel free to go to yogasimpleandsacred.com or yogaandgrief.com to download the audio versions of the Guided Meditation and Meditation for Relaxation (page 80).

longer practice

This section takes postures that you have previously learned and combines them into a longer practice. You will want to wear loose comfortable clothing and refrain from eating approximately two hours before starting. As you familiarize yourself with the sequence, you may want to hold the last repetition of each posture for a few breaths.

1. Abdominal Breath: Place hands on your abdomen and inhale the breath deep into your abdomen. On the exhalation, move your navel toward your spine. Repeat six times. When you become more comfortable with all the postures, you may want to practice abdominal breathing throughout this series, remembering to inhale and exhale through your nose.

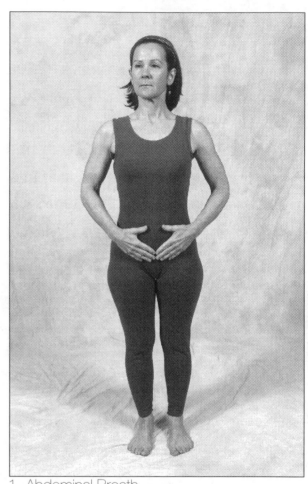

1. Abdominal Breath

2. Arm Raises (a)

2. Arm Raises (b)

2. Arm Raises: Stand with your arms by your sides. Inhale as you raise your arms out in front with bent elbows. Exhale to starting position. Repeat six times.

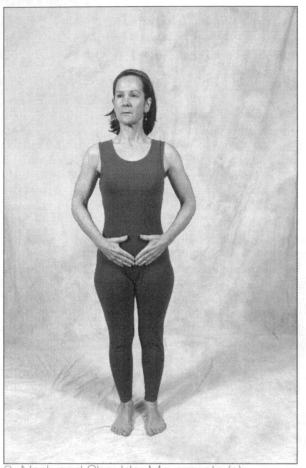

3. Neck and Shoulder Movements (a)

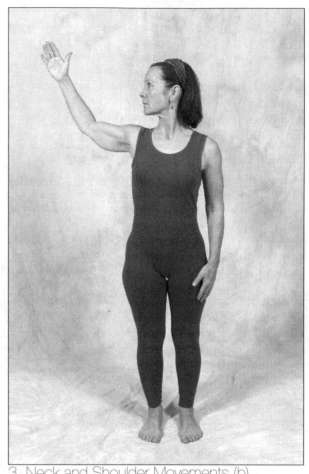

3. Neck and Shoulder Movements (b)

3. Neck and Shoulder Movements: Place your hands on your abdomen, allowing your eyes and head to follow the movement of your hand. Inhale while raising your right arm up and out to the side, elbow slightly bent. Exhale slowly, placing your hand on your left shoulder. Inhale as you take your arm up and out to the side again. Exhale as you bring your arm back to your abdomen. Alternate sides, three times.

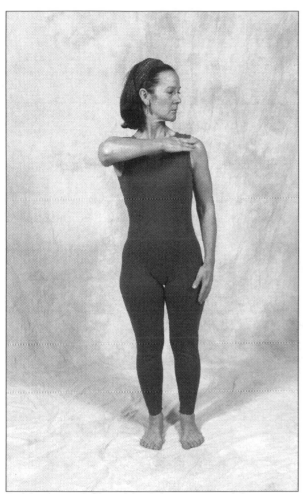

3. Neck and Shoulder Movements (c)

3. Neck and Shoulder Movements (d)

4. Balancing Posture (a)

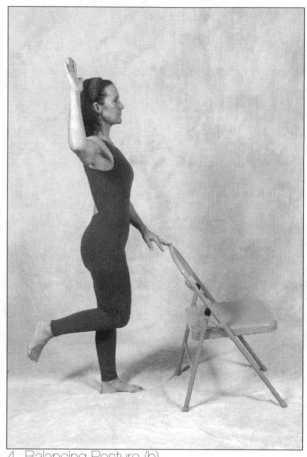

4. Balancing Posture (b)

4. Balancing Posture: Stand with your hands on the back of a chair. Inhale as you lift your right leg behind you and your right arm overhead having a slightly bent elbow. Exhale to starting position. Alternate sides, and repeat four more times. The last time, hold the posture for three breaths on each side. If you feel steady, you do not need to use the chair.

5. Warrior I (a)

5. Warrior I (b)

5. Warrior I: Step your right foot forward in a long stance. As you inhale, lift your arms up with elbows bent while bending your front knee. Watch that your knee does not go forward over your ankle. Exhale as you lower your arms and straighten your front leg. Repeat six times each side.

6. Standing Twist (a)

6. Standing Twist (b)

6. Standing Twist: Take a wide stance. As you inhale, raise your arms out to a T-position. With your gaze following your left hand, exhale and begin to turn your trunk to the left, allowing your right hand to come toward your left shoulder. As you inhale, come back to center. Exhale and repeat on the other side. Repeat each side three times. Remember to keep your back straight and your chin parallel to the floor.

7. Forward Bend (a)

7. Forward Bend (b)

7. Forward Bend: Start with your arms at your sides. Inhale as you raise your arms up with bent elbows. Exhale as you bend at the hips and allow your hands to slide down the front of your legs to a comfortable position, letting your head relax. Keeping your chin slightly tucked, inhale as you lift your chest as you come up slowly, letting your hands slide up your legs. Repeat four to six times. This can also be done with your hands resting on the seat of a chair.

8. **Rest:** Lie on your back with your knees bent, soles of feet on the floor or with legs straight out on the floor. Take three to five Three-part Breaths and then continue with the next posture.

9. Spinal Movements (a)

9. Spinal Movements (b)

9. Spinal Movements (c)

9. Spinal Movements: Come to your hands and knees, shoulders in line with wrists. Use padding for your knees, if necessary. Exhale as you move your hips back toward — but not onto — your heels. As you inhale, lead with your chest, moving forward and coming into a slight back arch. Repeat six times.

10. Leg Raises (a)

10. Leg Raises: Lie on your back with knees bent, feet off the floor, hands on knees. Inhale as you straighten your legs upward and move your arms overhead. Or, you may keep your hands behind your knees if you need the support. Exhale as you draw the knees towards the chest, hands on your knees, back to starting position. Repeat six times.

10. Leg Raises (b)

11. Pelvic Lifts (a)

12. Knees In and Out (a)

11. Pelvic Lifts (b)

12. Knees In and Out (b)

11. Pelvic Lifts: Place feet slightly apart on the floor, hands resting on chest. Inhale as you open arms out to the side and press your feet into the floor, lifting your hips to a comfortable level. Exhale as you return to starting position. Gradually increase the height of the lift as you are able. Repeat six times.

12. Knees In and Out: Lift feet off the ground, placing hands on top of, or under, your knees. Exhale as you draw your knees toward your chest. Inhale as you return to starting position. Repeat six times.

13. Kneeling Forward Bend (a)

13. Kneeling Forward Bend (b)

13. Kneeling Forward Bend: Stand on your knees with your arms by your sides, knees placed hip width apart. Inhale as you raise your arms to the front. Exhale as you bring your hips toward your heels and bend your trunk forward, placing your hands and head on the floor in front of you. If your head does not touch the floor, use a pillow. Relax your elbows. Keep your chin slightly tucked. Inhale as you lift your arms and chest. Exhale as you lower your arms to your sides. Repeat six times. You can bring your hands to a chair if you can't reach the floor. If you can't be on your knees, do a Forward Bend using a chair (see pages 26).

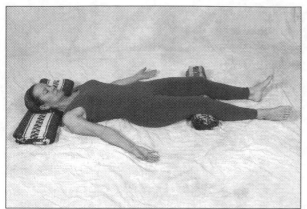

14. Relaxation Posture

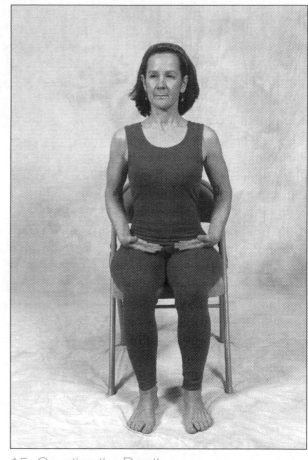

15. Counting the Breath

14. Relaxation Posture: Place a bolster or two folded blankets under your knees and a rolled towel or blanket under your neck. Relax with your arms by your sides. Give yourself at least five minutes in this posture. When you are done, bend your knees and slowly roll to your right side. Pause. Using your left hand for support, slowly come up, keeping your neck relaxed. Sit for a moment and take a few breaths. Notice what you feel.

15. Counting the Breath with Throat Breathing: Come to sitting in a chair. Count to yourself as your breath comes in and, again, as it goes out. Gradually try to extend your exhalation a couple of seconds longer than your inhalation. For example, inhale to the count of four and exhale to the count of six. Allow the back of your throat to constrict, narrowing the air passage so that you are making a sound like the ocean. When you are comfortable, add it to the inhalation. Eventually try to make your breath longer and smoother. Do two sets of six repetitions.

Just as the soft rains fill the streams,
Pour into the rivers and join together in the oceans,
so may the power of every moment of your goodness
flow forth to awaken and heal all beings,
Those here now, those gone before, those yet to come.

Traditional Buddhist chant

chanting

Chanting has been employed in nearly every culture and many religions for centuries as a means of increasing consciousness. Because of its repetitive nature, chanting also can be beneficial in bringing focus during times when the mind is agitated or when troubling thoughts consume us. It can redirect our energy from distraction and preoccupation and bring us to a state of tranquility. In addition, the sound of our own voice can be surprisingly reassuring and comforting.

When we say "chant," we are referring to rhythmic sound in the form of syllables or words. Chanting can be done in any language and may be aligned with any spiritual practice that is important to you. This method of using the voice to focus the mind allows us to be present in the moment. In itself, chanting can invoke a sense of reverence and allow the expression of positive feelings such as praise, gratitude, and wonder.

benefits

- Expands and lengthens the breath
- Improves concentration
- Calms the mind
- Serves as a tool for spiritual practice/ links the mind to a higher consciousness
- Balances emotions

I found that during my mother's illness, chanting allowed me to go inward and be calm. I was never one to feel comfortable singing, but chanting is different. I was comforted hearing the sound of my own voice in the midst of a very difficult time. The feeling of self-consciousness left me and I was even able to chant for my mother. The words, "Spirit, hear her, guide her, guide her, guide her now", became a prayer asking for the highest good.
-Gloria

the practice of chanting

First, keep in mind that chanting is not a performance. It is a tool to allow you to move toward a focused and peaceful state of mind. If you feel self-conscious, try to find a quiet place to practice. Close the door and give yourself permission to make sound.

Any soothing sound will have an effect. Some people find it easy to use vowel sounds: A E I O U or simple syllables that have peaceful associations like AH, MA, HUM or SO. These sounds can invite a state of alertness and/or calm when chanted on an exhalation. After you have been practicing for a while, you will notice that as you chant, your breath will start to lengthen, and you will be able to sustain the chant for longer periods.

It is important to use chants that are soothing and pleasant for you. Listed at the end of this chapter are suggestions that you might find comforting, but feel free to come up with your own. There are many available recordings of various types of chants, including those found on Gloria's website, which is listed in the Resource section of this book.

Once you are comfortable with using your voice, you can chant out loud or silently, depending on the situation and your comfort level. We recommend that you begin by chanting aloud so you can hear your voice. This serves to redirect attention. We learn to listen and remember the sound of our own voice. Eventually, you may want to try chanting silently, which requires a deeper sense of focus; however, do not rush into silent recitation. Hear the chant first, appreciate the sound of your own voice, and feel comfortable. Gradually, as you are able to refine the focus of your mind, you can begin to chant in a softer voice and finally move toward silent chanting.

Each sound lasts as long as a comfortable exhalation. Refrain from extending the sound so far that you end up gasping for breath. It helps if you can develop a slow steady count in your head — maybe three or more beats to each sound depending on the length of your breath and the speed of your counting. As you become comfortable repeating the one syllable sound, you can use longer chants with multiple words or syllables. Some people may immediately prefer silent recitation, but we suggest a more gradual progression: out loud first three times, then repeating it softly three times, then repeating it silently three times. As with most contemplative practices, there is no rush, so slow down and chant with the breath.

Simply notice the effects. Notice the difference between the loud, soft, and silent chant. There is no right or wrong way. Simply observe how it makes you feel, knowing that each time, and in each way, it may be different.

As you are able to refine your practice, you may link chanting to something you want to call into your life or to something to which you aspire. For example, if you love the sun, you may want to use its qualities of brightness, warmth, steadiness, and reliability in the chant you create. The main thing is to make it *your* practice.

chanting with yoga postures

Using yoga or gentle movements as you chant gives the mind less chance to wander, and, again, helps to improve focus. Try chanting a few times without sound until you are accustomed to the movements. Feel free to sit or stand, keeping your spine straight. For each movement, the syllable is chanted during the entire exhalation phase. Begin with a simple sound. As your breath is able to lengthen, you can then start to increase the length of your chanting. Add repetitions and increase the complexity of the chant, if you desire. Remember to inhale through the nose and exhale through the mouth as you chant.

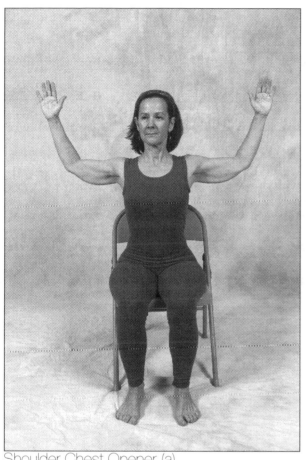

Shoulder Chest Opener (a)

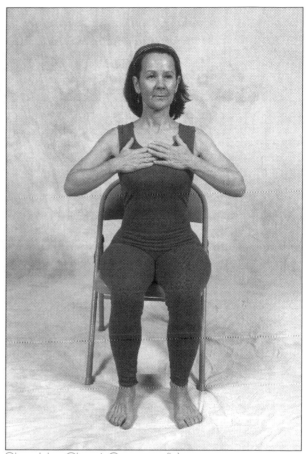

Shoulder Chest Opener (b)

Shoulder Chest Opener: This may also be done standing. Start with both hands at your chest. Inhale as you slightly lift the chest, opening your arms out to the side, elbows relaxed. Exhale while bringing your hands back to your chest. Repeat four to six times. Continue with the posture and, when ready, add a one-syllable sound to your exhalation. Your hands return to your heart at the end of the sound.

Neck and Shoulder Stretch (a)

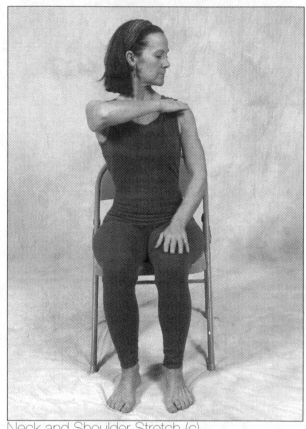

Neck and Shoulder Stretch (c)

Neck and Shoulder Stretch: Besides being a good gesture to accompany chanting, this is an excellent movement to help relieve tension in the neck and shoulders. In a sitting position place your hands in your lap. Inhale as you raise your right arm out to the side, elbow slightly bent. Allow your eyes and head to follow the movement of your hand. Exhale as you place your hand on your opposite shoulder. Inhale your arm out to the side again. Return your arms back to your lap. With each exhalation, use a chant of your choosing. Alternate sides. Repeat three times.

Neck and Shoulder Stretch (b)

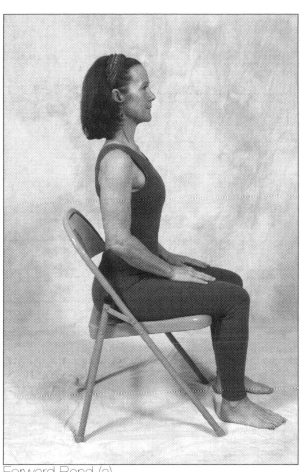

Forward Bend (a)

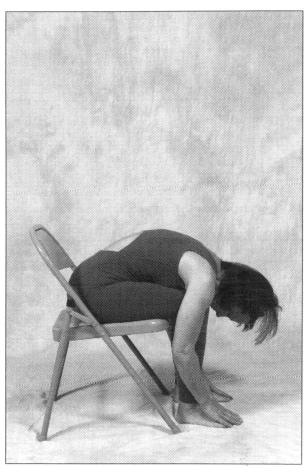

Forward Bend (b)

Forward Bend: Seated or standing, place hands on your lap. Exhale as you bend at the hips and allow your hands to slide down the front of your legs to a comfortable position. Keep your chin slightly tucked as you inhale, lifting your chest as you come up slowly, letting your hands slide up your legs. Chant on the exhalation, perhaps using "AH" or "MA." Repeat four to six times.

bear in mind
You may find it hard to stay focused when you are experiencing deep loss. Keep your practice simple, and remain aware of how you are feeling – physically and emotionally. Be patient and gentle with yourself. The chanting can comfort you and help you stay in the moment. Feel free to tailor your practice to what works best for you. Because chanting can slow you down and help you be in the moment, it is not surprising to feel strong emotions of grief and loss, or a flood of memories. It can also bring up feelings of happiness and serenity. And then again, it may not bring up anything at all. Notice how you feel when you chant — before, after, aloud, soft, or silent. Are there any changes? Whatever you feel or don't feel, it's where you need to be right now. Practicing acceptance can be a key to healing.

using chant in caring for another
Chanting can be used not only by the caregiver but also for the person receiving care. Chants, either recorded or live, may be a way to soothe a person in the time of transition. However it is very important to understand the situation and be attentive and respectful of the needs of others. Accept them where they are in their journey, and keep in mind that issues such as pain control or loss of function may be at odds with your own desire to help. At times, you may need to set aside your own ideas of what is helpful and provide care in other ways. Be mindful and patient with yourself and others. If there is an opportunity for chanting, always ask permission and make sure the content is relevant for the person.

one syllable sounds

A E I O U

AAH MA SO HUM HA AUM OM

word chants

ALLELUIA

AVE

PEACE/ CALM/ SERENITY*

OM SHANTI, SHANTI, SHANTI*

chant built on word or sound*

- Be still
- Be still and know
- Be still and know that I am
- Be still and know that I am God.

*Recordings of these chants can be found on Gloria's website at yogasimpleandsacred.com and yogaandgrief.com.

I had a long relationship with a dear friend and student who allowed me to participate in her care toward the end of her life. Chanting became a source of calm during our visits together and in the last days of her illness, when she could no longer chant aloud, she would listen and gain comfort from focusing on the sound and repeating it silently.

-Gloria

forgiving mistakes and moving forward

by Sonia Nelson
based on a Sanskrit Chant

With my best intentions still mistakes were made.

Please forgive these.

And through grace, may I remain on the path I've chosen.

Sustained by faith, strength,

the memory of my devotion.

The soil in which the meditative mind can begin is the soil of everyday life, the strife, the pain, and the fleeting joy. It must begin there and bring order, and from there, move endlessly.

Jiddu Krishnamurti

INDIAN PHILOSOPHER AND SPIRITUAL TEACHER

meditation

Meditation is another technique we can use to calm the mind and create an inner space where we can be free of worries and discomfort. As with chanting, meditation is an ancient practice that allows us to direct the mind and bring awareness to the present moment. Today, it is taught in a variety of settings from hospitals to corporate retreats as a way to improve focus, and foster relaxation and wellness. For some, prayer is also considered a form of meditation.

why meditate when you are grieving?

In times of grief and stress, you may find yourself lost, unable to keep to a routine and operating mechanically just to get through the day. You may have difficulty sleeping. The source of this stress may come from the past, dwelling on what has been lost, or in contemplating a future that is fearful and unknown. You forget, or maybe never learned, that you can only exist in the present moment. Meditation helps you live in the present by focusing on one moment at a time. It may help you put aside deep and intense emotions — regret, fearfulness, impatience, whatever it may be. If you can sit and ease your mind, relax for a short time, it may be most important thing you do for yourself all day. In and of itself, meditation will not take away pain, but it may help to ease it. It is not a quick fix, nor a way to anesthetize yourself from grief, but can be a source of peace that will enable you to continue on your journey of healing.

It may be hard to do something good for yourself when you are full of sorrow and sadness; however, this is the time to practice a little loving kindness toward yourself. It may mean that you take one breath and allow yourself to be free from thought for a moment. Perhaps you will be able to do this several times a day as you build mindfulness into your routine. You may have to force yourself at times to "just do it." You will feel better afterward. On those particular days, you may say, "I don't have to sit long, but I will sit."

to begin

Traditionally in yoga one would do a few yoga postures to prepare the body to be more open for sitting in meditation. However, for those shorter practices, it may not be as important. What matters is that you *do* it. There are many ways to meditate besides what we have suggested here. Feel free to investigate other techniques. What matters is that the approach is comfortable and allows you to make a commitment to your practice.

Meditation is about awareness, and it is easy for thoughts to take you out of awareness. Keep in mind that you are seeking a state that is non-judgmental. So when thoughts creep back in, simply honor and acknowledge them without judgment; let them go, and return to your meditation technique.

If you are new to meditation, begin gradually. Start with five minutes at a time, then steadily build up to 20 minutes or longer once you find a technique that fits for you. It may be helpful to set a timer for the minutes you want to sit; this way your mind doesn't become distracted wondering how much longer you have to meditate or if you'll sit too long.

In many traditions, morning and evening are the suggested times to meditate. You may do it in the morning before getting involved in the day's tasks; and in the evening before bedtime, when it may be helpful to calm the mind as well as the nervous system. Really, whenever you can do it is the best time for you.

sitting meditation
Many people feel most comfortable meditating in a seated position. As you begin your practice, it is important that your body be comfortable and your spine straight. Wear loose-fitting clothing, if possible. If you are uncomfortable in your body, your mind will go to the source of discomfort instead of to a state of peacefulness. If at any time you become uncomfortable, change your position, moving slowly and with a sense of awareness.

Sit on the floor, by a wall, or in a chair. If you are sitting on the floor you can sit on a cushion or blanket with the legs crossed and the knees lower than the hips. The chin is parallel to the floor. Allow the spine to be straight so your breathing is unrestricted. Focus with your eyes barely open or closed, depending upon your preference. The hands can rest in the lap, palms up, and the elbows slightly bent, or you can use one of the hand gestures discussed later in this chapter.

breathing and meditation

Paying attention to your breathing can be a useful tool for focusing the mind. First observe the breath as it rises and falls. Abdominal Breathing with Throat Breathing on pages 14-16 is a good technique to use.

You can focus your breath by placing your hands on the abdomen one above the other and inhale the breath deep into the abdomen. On the exhalation, move the navel toward the spine. Observe the breath coming into and out of the abdomen. If you do notice thoughts coming in, just observe them and come back to the breath until the thought plays itself out. Let it be. Don't engage. Let the thoughts pass like clouds.

using mudras Hand

gestures, or *mudras*, help change the energy flow of the body and focus the mind inward. In Sanskrit, *mudra* means "to seal." You can add any of the following *mudras* to the meditation techniques listed.

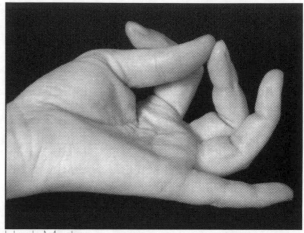
Hook Mudra

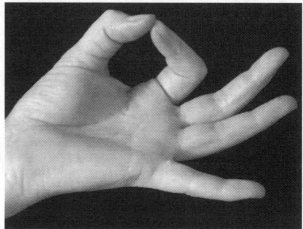
Jñana Mudra

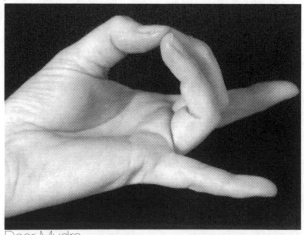
Deer Mudra

Hook Mudra: Helps to focus the mind. Palms placed facing upward on lap; the index finger comes in front, hooking over the knuckle of the thumb, and the pad of the middle finger and the thumb come together.

Jñana Mudra: To invoke balance, help the nervous system and for concentration and meditation. Place the thumb and index finger of both hands together, palms facing up on your lap.

Deer Mudra: For protection. The pads of the thumb, middle and ring fingers of each hand come together while the index and little fingers are kept straight with the palms up.

focusing on an object

This could be a photo of something that comforts you, an icon of your favorite saint or deity, a flower floating in a bowl, or a lit candle. When you find the mind wandering off, focus again on the image. You may incorporate any of the breathing techniques that give you comfort while looking at the image.

walking meditation

Some people prefer walking meditation as their regular practice. Others may find it most helpful when the mind and body are especially restless. This type of meditation may help to calm you by giving your mind more than one function on which to focus. The same is true if you add a hand mudra or chant to your practice.

Begin by slowly walking heel to toe, observing each step you take and bringing awareness to your action. When the mind wanders off, come back to feeling each step as you are taking it. This can be done outdoors in nature, in your own backyard, or even in the house. You can use a chant and/or a hand gesture as well to help you stay present.

Another walking meditation technique is to notice everything in your path as you walk: "There is a rock," "There is a yellow flower," "There is a blue bicycle." You don't go into the details; you simply notice the things along the path without any comment or story attached. Stay in the moment. Keep coming back to what you notice.

Though it was already part of my daily activities, meditation became a life saver with each visit I made to see and care for my mom. It was a source of quiet help that allowed me to really be with her and participate in her care.

When the end was near, I found occasional moments of respite away from the hospital, being outdoors, sitting or walking, breathing, meditating. Feeling the softness of my fingertips as they came together in a mudra, the deliberate steps of my feet touching the earth grounded me when the days got really hard.

-Gloria

labyrinth
walk Walking the spiral pathway

of a labyrinth is another way to incorporate movement into meditation. Its geometric shape may be constructed from a variety of materials such as stone, brick, or living plants. Other names for a labyrinth are mandala or a medicine wheel. Some have existed since pre-historic times, some are found in churches; others, in nature. By focusing on walking the curved path of a labyrinth you are gently guided on a symbolic pilgrimage toward enlightenment. A profound sense of opening and release can result from this type of walking meditation practice. The website, www.labyrinthlocator.com maintains a directory of labyrinths around the world and makes it easy to find one in your area.

Walking a labyrinth may be interpreted as a way to let go of something -- perhaps letting go of fear and sorrow, or an attachment to the desire that things be different. With that letting go, you may begin to hear the inner self speak with a greater sense of clarity.

As you approach the labyrinth, allow the mind to empty into silence as you would with any meditation. If you feel nothing right after the walk, or think that nothing has changed, give yourself some time. In Gloria's grief workshops a number of people have remarked that they received new clarity and insight even days after their walk.

Here is one way to approach a labyrinth.

Entering: Take a moment to pause and bow in gratitude, or say a prayer for the journey you are about to begin. If other people are walking the labyrinth, simply step to the side to let the person pass.

Walking: You may choose to use either of the suggestions from Walking Meditation: heel-to-toe walking, or observing everything in your path as a way to calm the "monkey mind," the mental chatter.

Center: This is a place of contemplation. Stay a while and take time to notice how you feel. Receive what this time has to offer you. Ask for clarity and insight. You may notice that some people leave an offering. Feel free to do the same, considering it as a token of appreciation.

Journey Outward: Reflect on what occurred in the center. Observe what manifests as you walk outward. See what comes to you when your mind is peaceful and receptive.

Leaving: To complete the meditation, turn and face the labyrinth in gratitude.

Take time to reflect on your experience. Notice how you feel just after completing the labyrinth and, perhaps, in the days that follow.

the rewards

In meditation, again and again, remember to come back to a peaceful mind. When you have completed your practice, try to maintain awareness of your meditative mind throughout the rest of your day. The benefits may be surprising. Maybe for the first time you see a flower, a cloud, or the face of a child in a more vivid and yet peaceful, way. These are the gifts of living, the moments that illuminate the spiritual connection to something greater than ourselves.

guided meditation

Some people find that the voice of another is helpful to achieve a meditative state. Audio meditations like the ones you can find at yogaandgrief.com can be used to help with sleep problems, feelings of anxiety, heaviness, or a sense of hopelessness, or simply to relax.

Listen to each meditation. You might prefer having them read to you. Each one lasts approximately ten minutes. Perhaps you could play soft music in the background. Make sure you are comfortable. Turn off the phone. Avoid interruptions. Pause frequently. Relax.

Find a comfortable position in bed or on the floor, supporting the neck and back of the knees, if you desire.

meditation for relaxation This

is an especially good technique for relaxation after your yoga practice or any time to de-stress.

Begin by observing the breath. Simply notice the inhalation and exhalation. No need to change anything about the breath, simply notice it.

Bring your awareness to your feet and toes. Feel your toes by wiggling them. Let the feet relax into the support beneath you.

Sense your calf muscles and relax both the right and left side.

Now relax the front and back of the legs entirely.

Feel how limp and loose they are; how relaxed they feel.

Gently move your awareness to the back of your body, your buttocks, and the lower and upper back. Readjust if you are not completely comfortable.

The entire back part of your body is relaxed into your support.

Now the awareness moves to the front of the body.

Allow the muscles of the chest and abdomen to soften with your breath.

The organs relax inside you.

Your breathing is peaceful, and relaxed.

Find comfort in the breath and allow it to support you as you relax even deeper.

Your arms are relaxed, and your fingers go

soft.

Move your awareness to the back of your neck.

Turn the head slightly side-to-side to find the most relaxing position.

Let there be no strain or tension in the neck or shoulders. If so, readjust your position.

The breath comes in. The breath goes out.

The mouth is slightly open, teeth slightly separated. You may swallow to release any tension in the throat.

The jaw is relaxed and loose.

Eyes fall back into their sockets. The eyelids are relaxed.

The muscles of the forehead are softening.

Release any remaining tension that you observe in the body.

The mind is empty of thoughts.

Give yourself permission to fully and completely relax.

If waves of emotions or thoughts filter in, simply witness them and allow them to be released.

Now the mind and body are fully relaxed.

There is nothing to do,

nowhere to go.

There is only this state of complete relaxation.

Stay here as long as you need. When ready, slowly transition to a seated position, giving yourself a few minutes to get grounded.

meditation on the breath

Notice the breath as it enters at the tip of your nose, moving down into the chest, then into the abdomen.

As you exhale, notice the breath emptying out from the abdomen, then the chest, then the nose.

Observe how slow or fast the breath enters and leaves the body.

Again, notice the breath as it enters at the tip of your nose, moving down into the chest, then into the abdomen.

Now begin to let the exhalation be longer than the inhalation by a second or two.

Do not force the inhalation or the exhalation.

If the mind wanders off, gently come back to the breath.

Inhale through the nose, down into the chest and abdomen.

Gently, follow the exhalation out of the abdomen, chest, and nose.

The exhalation is a little longer than the

inhalation.

If, at any time, there is a feeling of agitation or constriction in the breath, go back to your normal breathing pattern. When you are able, come back to watching the breath as it enters and leaves the body.

Allow slow inhalations and even slower exhalations.

Know that it is the mind's job to think and wander off.

Do not resist your thoughts. Merely observe them, and let them float away like the clouds in the sky.

Remember the exhalation is a bit longer than the inhalation.

The awareness is at the tip of your nose as you inhale, moving the breath down into the chest, then into the abdomen.

Exhale the breath out from the abdomen, then the chest, then the nose.

The body is completely relaxed, yet alert.

You are watching the breath as it enters and leaves the body.

When you are ready, release control of the breath and return to your normal breathing pattern.

Stay here if you need more time then when you are ready, slowly come back into your surroundings. Sit for a moment. Take some slow, long breaths in and out. Reflect. Be with whatever feeling or thoughts that may be present for you. Take a moment to express gratitude for your wellness and this time to nurture yourself.

The audio version of these guided meditations may be found on the Yoga Sacred and Simple website at yogasimpleandsacred. com and yogaandgrief.com.

Start by doing what is necessary, then what is possible,
and suddenly you are doing the impossible.

St. Francis of Assisi

CATHOLIC SAINT

seeking comfort

ritual and comfort

For a number of years, Gloria has offered grief workshops as a component of *Yoga Simple and Sacred*. These workshops present opportunities to deal with loss and grief in a supportive and peaceful environment. Though each journey is different, we all learn something from each other. We explore forgiveness, for ourselves and others. We are safe to unload the burden of our feelings. Sometimes we may even come to terms with our suffering. We can do this through the rituals of yoga, meditation, and ceremony.

In the *Yoga Simple and Sacred* grief workshops, ritual is a significant part of the healing process. By ritual we mean symbolic, ceremonial acts that create sacred space. Yoga, focused breathing and meditation can be forms of ritual. There are, in addition, rituals that have personal meaning beyond these practices. They are acts that mark change or turning points in our lives. They can support us in times of uncertainty and vulnerability. They may bring peace or deep spiritual awakening. Ritual can create a shelter from the chaos and allows communication with the unknown, the untapped energy that some might call the divine.

At some point in the grieving process, you may find yourself wanting to create personal rituals or ceremonies. You may do it to bring focus or closure, to celebrate and renew, or to purge negativity. Incense and music may be incorporated as well as any religious or spiritual practices that have meaning for you. Ceremonies can be performed whenever you feel you are ready. They can be performed alone or you can invite others to participate. Your ritual could be something as simple as sending an email to loved ones to commemorate a particular time with a collective thought or prayer. It is your journey, so create what you need.

Here are a few techniques that have helped others.

healing rituals

writing and meditation

Sit in prayer, meditation, or stillness. Have a pen and journal handy. During deeply quiet and reflective times you may gain insights or clarity. If you do, write it down. Or pose a question about something that has remained unresolved and listen for the response through your meditation.

Do not judge the content of what you write or critique your style. Let the words flow. If the process gets painful, take full deep breaths or stop, if necessary. You might ask what your loved one would say to you now. You could pose a question and then listen. You may be very surprised with what comes of these sessions.

In one of my meditation sessions after the death of my mother when I was having thoughts that I could have done more or been a better daughter, I received the impression that she would have said, "I will forgive you, if you forgive me...."

-Gloria

Turn off the internal critic. Let go of the chatter. Feel the flow. It is your unconscious manifesting within you.

letters and photographs

Letter writing can be a great release for those expressions that may have been left unsaid. A letter of forgiveness is a way to address the hurt. Maybe you didn't get a chance to say: "I love you," "I miss you," "I am sorry," "I forgive you," or even "Goodbye." You may choose to preserve this letter in a special way, or you might choose to burn it as an offering. Perhaps you could wrap the letter and some photos or mementos with flowers tucked in between the pages and place them in a small fire pit. As you light the paper bundle you may wish to say a prayer or give a blessing as the smoke rises to the heavens.

eulogy

Gloria decided to write a eulogy for her mom when she was in hospice. She took a little time each day while she was with her to reflect and write what she meant to her. She wrote down the funny things and the endearing moments. The priest who officiated at her service used some of what she wrote to help make his own comments reflect Gloria's mother's life and personality.

Eulogy can be done in many different ways. It can be formal or informal. It can even be a powerful exercise to explore thoughts and feelings for our loved ones who are still alive. As Gloria was writing the eulogy for her mom she thought, "Why wait until they are gone to let my brothers and sisters know how they have touched my life?" So she wrote a kind of eulogy for each of them, and then one for herself.

dream journal

"Every dream we have of a loved one who has passed can move us toward healing," a presenter once said in a workshop. No matter how short the dream or how much you can remember, write it down. Keep the journal by your bedside so you can immediately record your dreams or thoughts without disturbing the mood. Later, if you chose to review what you have written, you may find some insight. Notice your mood when you awaken, even if you may not recall the dream. You might feel a release, or the heart may feel heavy. The main thing is not to judge the process and to be respectful of what you feel.

Some nights Gloria felt such deep sorrow and the need to see, hear, touch her mom again. She asked her mom to visit in her dreams. She would request this in her evening prayers. Tillie would appear sometimes with Gloria's dad. Sometimes she was healthy, other times ill. When she appeared sick, Gloria took it as a sign that helped her be thankful that she was no longer suffering. Many times she felt gratitude because she got to see and talk to her. The message from these visits was: "Believe in what comforts you." This may not work for everyone, so don't feel bad if you cannot do it.

a list of attributes

A healing ritual

to stay focused when you are experiencing deep loss can be performed by listing qualities that you appreciated about your loved one. For example, in some cultures, the number 108 is considered auspicious. Perhaps you could try listing 108 attributes. You might decide to spend months or years on such a project. It doesn't have to be 108 – simply start a list of appreciations.

collage It may take some time

before you are ready for this, but if you have access to photos, making a collage is a wonderful way to reminisce and celebrate a person's life.

You may want to set aside a separate day to go through photos and to pick out the ones that speak to you. Include pictures of special events, such as marriage, births, family gatherings, and holidays. If you need more, ask family and friends to send you copies. You can also use keepsakes such as a small piece of jewelry, invitations, letters, or postcards. The basics are photos, mementos, glue stick, scissors, and poster board. If you make it a standard size, you can put it in a ready-made frame.

Or you might prefer to create a computer slide show, a photo book, or photo magnets. Any of these can be copied and sent to family and friends.

Before starting, sit quietly and form an intention. For example, ask that the project help with healing, and for celebrating that person's life. You might play music that reminds you of the person, or light a candle and say a prayer. Ask that you might be open to receive the gifts of your actions. Without judging, allow yourself to be open to your creative energy. Make it a time of love and remembrance. When you are done, you may feel both exhausted and powerful.

healing bodywork Because

tension can manifest in physical ways during difficult times, bodywork is very useful to maintain energy and care for oneself. This is especially true if you are providing care during the transition of a loved one.

There are also other types of bodywork, so find something that suits your needs and comfort level. You may benefit from chiropractics or other treatments that can align the body. Massage is another excellent way to relieve stress. If you never have had a massage, or if you are feeling vulnerable, a chair massage may be the way to start. Or you may opt for energy work such as reiki, shiatsu or cranial-sacral. In these modalities, you remain fully clothed.

Keep in mind that you may have to do a little searching to find the right person to match your needs. It is not unreasonable to expect to find someone loving and nurturing, but it may not happen the first time. Don't give up. While you don't have to process your grief with that person, you do need to feel comfortable. With any type of bodywork, it is important to let the practitioner know how you are feeling or that you may have the need to cry. They should be comfortable with such a request.

suggestions from the yoga and grief workshops

In the Yoga and Grief workshops, Gloria and the participants generate a lot of discussion about the things that make them feel better. Some are physical objects and some are activities that we have discussed elsewhere in this book:

soothing body and mind

Yoga

Breathing exercises

Massage

Walking/ biking/ swimming

Meditation/prayer

Talking to a friend/finding support

Being in nature/watching sunrises and sunsets

Movement/dance

Housework

soothing the senses

Playing or listening to music

Calming aromatherapy, such as rose or lavender water sprayed on pillows before bedtime

Caring for a pet

Warm baths with mineral salts

Homeopathic/Bach remedies

creative acts

Creating an altar

Journaling/creative writing/letter writing

Keeping a dream notebook

Participating in Day of the Dead activities

These events are often celebrated in Latin American communities in early November. Altars are erected honoring departed loved ones, and the festivities may include parades and community celebrations.

Planting flowers or trees as memorials

Hi Gloria,

Guess what? I loved the image and symbol of the flowers coming up in the spring each year. You shared this in one of our grief classes. So toward the end of fall, I bought some bulbs and I planted, and planted, and planted (very therapeutic!) and over the past few weeks, it has been nothing short of a miracle to see the tulips and daffodils and hyacinths push up through the hard earth. It gives me such joy to water them and to see the changes each day. Thank you for such a great idea.

-Julie

a few words about food
We have talked about many techniques that we can do to feel better, and one of the most important is healthy eating. Stress can affect our eating patterns: Some of us may feel we cannot eat, while others of us may eat more than usual. This, in turn, affects our moods and physical well-being.

Focusing on a well-balanced diet and keeping the empty calories to a minimum will help. However, as with all good intentions, there are times when you can't avoid temptation. For example, ice cream may be calling to you. It's okay. Eat it and love every bite, while trying to do so in moderation.

The acts of eating and preparing food can be meditative. You may find that friends and family try to comfort you by bringing a meal. The hardest part might be asking or allowing people to help. It's okay to receive. You may return the favor someday.

As we mentioned at the beginning, many people going through loss may experience illness themselves. Maintaining your strength and nourishing your body will, in turn, nourish your mind and reduce stress.

final words

Loss and grief teaches us that sorrow can be isolating. For that reason, we hope this book may provide comfort and support to you, knowing that we will all experience grief at some point in life. In time, may hope be rekindled and your heart be peaceful as you continue the compassionate journey toward healing.

We wish you well.

resources

DESIKACHAR, T.K.V. *The Heart of Yoga:Developing a Personal Practice.* Rochester, VT: Inner Traditions International, 1995. www.InnerTraditions.com, www.kym.org/

HARVEY, Paul. *Yoga for Every Body.* New York: Readers' Digest 2001.

KABAT-ZINN, Jon, Ph.D. *Full Catastrophe Living: Using the Wisdom of Your Body and Mind to Face Stress, Pain, and Illness.* New York: Delta, 1990.

LEVINE, STEPHEN. *Guided Meditations, Explorations and Healing.* New York: Anchor, 1991.

PIERCE, MARGARET AND MARTIN. *Yoga for Your Life.* New York: Sterling Publishing Co., 1999.

gloria's websites

www.yogasimpleandsacred.com

www.yogaandgrief.com

Gloria Drayer, R.Y.T. *Yoga Simple and Sacred*

chanting

Vedic Chant Center, Santa Fe, New Mexico

Sonia Nelson, director

www.vedicchantcenter.org

labyrinths

www.labyrinthlocator.com

magazines

Living with Loss© Magazine

Bereavement Publications, Inc. Eckert, CO

www.livingwithloss.com

acknowledgments

To all who have helped and encouraged us in the writing and production of this book, especially,

Jon Aase,

Sonia Nelson,

Laura Feldberg,

Nicholas Aase,

Sue Houser,

Polly Robinson,

Bonita Ferus, for her chanting and the use of her recording studio,

Jutta Lehmer, web designer, auroradesign.us

Carolyn Flynn, cover and interior design, SoulFireStudios writing coaching, editing and design; transformational and creative strategy consulting, carolynflynn.com.

Barbara Conley, photographer

Molly Shannon, photographer, serenityhousequilting.shutterfly.com,

Mela Chapman, photographer

Jodi Newton, photographer, jodinewton.com

Jerry Sue Bassalleck, photographer

All who have participated in the yoga and grief workshops, to teachers and students, past and present, who have helped spread the message of yoga; and to Gloria's sisters and brothers for their help in caring for their mother.

about the authors

Kathleen Doherty is a former hospice nurse, clinical research manager, and student of Gloria's since 2005. Along the way she has learned that a grief observed is not the same as a grief experienced.

She has relied on the concepts of this book – yoga, meditation, and breathing techniques to appreciate days, dark and light. She lives in Albuquerque, New Mexico.

Gloria Drayer is known for the intuition, empathy, and compassion she brings to Yoga Simple and Sacred, her life-affirming approach to yoga retreats, workshops and classes. A certified yoga instructor, she teaches international yoga retreats, as well as weekly classes in Albuquerque, New Mexico. Workshops focus on life-transforming topics such as grief and loss, soul-enhancing approaches such as Full Moon Yoga and Winter/Summer Solstice Yoga, as well as physical challenges such as insomnia and menopause. She has lived and taught at Kripalu, the country's largest yoga and holistic health center located in Massachusetts, and holds a 500-hour certification with Kripalu and Yoga Alliance. Having studied at the Krishnamacharya Yoga Mandiram, Gloria is influenced by the teaching tradition of T.K.V. Desikachar and Prof. T. Krishnamacharya. She continues her studies with Sonia Nelson.
Find out more about Gloria at yogasimpleandsacred.com. and yogaandgrief.com

Excerpts from this book were published in the Summer 2010 print edition
and the January 2011 e-magazine of *Living with Loss Magazine*.

Sonia Nelson's *Chant for Forgiving Mistakes and Moving Forward* is used with permission.